WITHDRAWAL

MILITARY SPECIAL OPS

AIR
COMMANDOS

ELITE OPERATIONS

BY MARCIA AMIDON LUSTED

Lerner Publications Company
Minneapolis

Lerner Publications Company
A division of Lerner Publishing Group, Inc.
241 First Avenue North
Minneapolis, MN 55401 U.S.A.

Website address: www.lernerbooks.com

Content Consultant: Kalev Sepp, assistant professor, Naval Postgraduate School

Library of Congress Cataloging-in-Publication Data
Lusted, Marcia Amidon.
     Air commandos : elite operations / by Marcia Amidon Lusted.
          pages   cm. — (Military special ops)
     Includes index.
     ISBN 978–0–7613–9081–7 (lib. bdg. : alk. paper)
     ISBN 978–1–4677–1761–8 (eBook)
     1. United States. Air Force—Commando troops—Juvenile literature.
I. Title.
UG633.L77 2014
356'.16—dc23   2012048177

Manufactured in the United States of America
1 — MG — 7/15/13

The images in this book are used with the permission of: U.S. Air Force, 5, 8, 19; © USAF/AP Images, 6; Staff Sergeant Ernest H. Sealing/U.S. National Archives, 11; Master Sgt. Jeremy Lock/U.S. Air Force, 13, 29; Christopher Callaway/ U.S. Air Force, 14; David Salanitri/U.S. Air Force, 15; MSGT James M. Bowman/U.S. Air Force, 16; Staff Sgt. Julianne M. Showalter/U.S. Air Force, 20; Master Sgt. Lance Cheung/U.S. Air Force, 21; Staff Sgt. Christopher Marasky/U.S. Air Force, 23; Senior Airman Ali Flisek/U.S. Air Force, 25; Master Sgt. Russell E Cooley IV/U.S. Air Force, 26; Airman 1st Class Christopher Williams/U.S. Air Force, 27; John Hughel/Air National Guard, 28.

Front cover: U.S. Air Force photo/Tech. Sgt. James L. Harper Jr.

Main body text set in Tw Cen MT Std Medium 12/18.
Typeface provided by Adobe Systems.

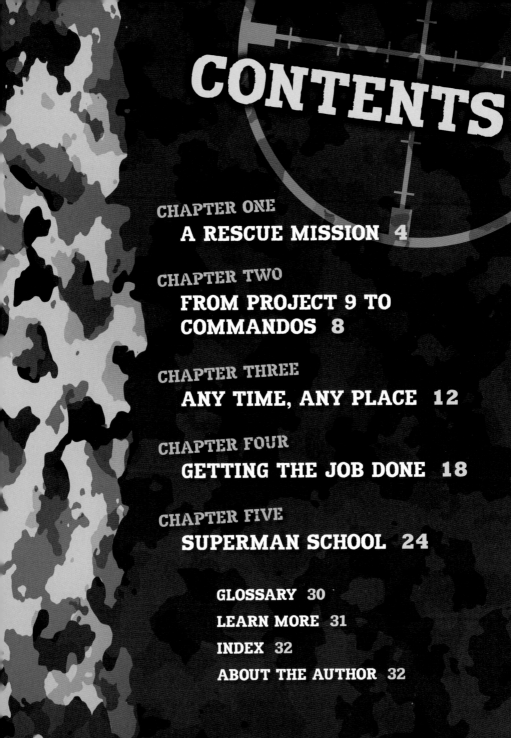

CONTENTS

CHAPTER ONE: A RESCUE MISSION

The cold winter wind swept across the hills of Balkh Province, Afghanistan. It was January 2012. A unit of the U.S. Air Force Special Operations Command (AFSOC), known as the Air Commandos, was helping with an army helicopter attack. The target was a group of Taliban rebels. The rebels had been building different types of bombs. They were using their homemade bombs against U.S. and Afghan military forces and civilians. The rebels were hiding in a group of caves. They were only 330 feet (100 meters) from the Air Commandos' position.

The captain of the Air Commandos was acting as the combat controller. His unit set up the assault with two U.S. Army attack

COMBAT CONTROLLERS

Combat controllers (CCTs) guide the safe landing of aircraft during combat actions. They set up military airfields. They send different signals to keep aircraft on course. They have to know about navigation tools, including flares, smoke grenades, and rotating beacons. And they have to know a variety of combat techniques too. It takes fifteen extra weeks of special training to become a CCT.

A CCT in Afghanistan watches out for enemy forces.

helicopters. The helicopters fired at the caves. At the same time, the Air Commandos on the ground moved toward the enemy's position. Rebels inside the caves were shooting at them. One of the Air Commandos was wounded while clearing a nearby building. He was a medic who had been helping injured Afghan women and children.

The Air Commandos' captain bravely ran through enemy fire to rescue the wounded medic. The rebels were only a few feet away from the captain. He threw a smoke grenade into the cave to blind the enemy. Then he dragged the medic to safety. Two Afghan soldiers working with the U.S. airmen were shot too. The fighting briefly stopped. It was enough time for the Air Commandos to move the wounded away from the enemy position.

AFSOC ORGANIZATION

AFSOC includes groups such as Special Operations Wings and Special Tactics units. Air Commandos are members of these groups. Special Operations Wings are made up of pilots and support crew. They specialize in counterterrorism, rescue and resupply in combat areas, and supporting ground units. Special Tactics units include combat controllers, pararescue jumpers, meteorologists, and communications personnel. Special Tactics units are often the first on the ground in combat situations.

An Air Commando (*left*) stands guard as an Afghan ally communicates by radio.

The Air Commandos then prepared a landing area for helicopters south of the cave. They had to find a flat spot among the area's steep mountain slopes and deep valleys. They cleared it of brush, trees, and large rocks. The wounded men were evacuated. The rest of the Air Commando unit moved to a safe distance from the caves. Then a U.S. Air Force bomber dropped a precision-guided bomb on the enemy cave complex. Both the caves and the rebels inside were destroyed.

Air Commandos don't usually get a lot of attention. But they perform very important jobs. They spend as much time helping the U.S. Army and Navy as they do the U.S. Air Force. Some are combat controllers. Others are pararescue jumpers, called PJs for short. Others are meteorologists. Still others pilot combat aircraft. Without them, other military groups would have trouble getting themselves behind enemy lines. It would be harder for them to get supplies or support during battles. And their wounded soldiers would not be rescued as quickly. Air Commandos are special because they must have many different skills. This makes the unit very difficult to join. But it also makes the Air Commandos one of the most important units in the entire U.S. military.

PARARESCUE JUMPERS

Pararescue jumpers are emergency medics. They parachute behind enemy lines to find wounded soldiers. Their mission is to be first on the scene when a plane goes down or when a natural disaster strikes. They are rescue experts in every environment—air, land, and sea. They are skilled in everything from parachuting to scuba diving. Their motto is That Others May Live. The best PJs in the air force serve on Special Tactics teams.

CHAPTER TWO:
FROM PROJECT 9 TO COMMANDOS

World War II (1939–1945) proved airplanes were one of the U.S. military's best weapons. Airplanes that could fly high and far were thought to be the most important. But commanders soon realized that airplanes to fly low over battle areas were needed too. These aircraft could drop soldiers behind enemy lines for surprise attacks. In 1943 U.S. Army Air Corps general Henry "Hap" Arnold created Project 9. It was an air support group for Allied forces on the

World War II–era Air Commandos flew this C-47 airplane, sometimes called the Gooney Bird.

ground. The project was soon renamed the First Air Commandos Group. During World War II, these Air Commandos flew low over Japanese-occupied territory. They backed up ground troops with firepower and supplies. They delivered food and additional soldiers and rescued wounded men.

In 1947 the U.S. Air Force became a separate military branch. It was no longer part of the army. During the Korean War (1950–1953), Air Commandos attacked the enemy. They dropped fighters behind enemy lines. But the Vietnam War (1957–1975) really showed how important the Air Commandos are. Starting in 1961, they helped the air force fight in new ways. The Air Commandos flew airplanes that could fire machine guns and cannon from the air. They helped troops on the ground trapped by enemy soldiers. The Air Commandos trained special pararescue jumpers as the air force began using more helicopters.

VIETNAM WAR AIRCRAFT

One specially outfitted airplane the Air Commandos used during the Vietnam War was the AC-47 Spooky. It was also called Puff the Magic Dragon. This C-47 cargo plane was modified to carry three multibarrel machine guns. These guns could shoot six thousand bullets per minute through their revolving barrels. The three guns pointed out of the left side of the airplane. When the pilot circled an area where there was fighting, the guns could be fired continuously on the same target.

In 1980 U.S. military forces tried to rescue American hostages held inside Iran. Air Commandos from the 1st Special Operations Wing played a role in this mission, called Operation Eagle Claw. But these airmen were not highly trained in flying helicopters low over the desert at night. When the rescue force stopped at night to refuel on its way to where the hostages were imprisoned, one helicopter collided with an airplane, destroying the aircraft and killing eight Americans. The rescue mission had to be called off.

The United States realized it needed to strengthen its special operations forces after the failure of Operation Eagle Claw. Changes were made to the equipment and roles of the Air Commandos. Their headquarters and airplanes were transferred to Hurlburt Field in Florida. More money was provided for specialized aircraft and training. The Air Commandos were soon qualified to support any branch of the military. They would play an important role in Operation Desert Storm

MISSION IN FOCUS — OPERATION EAGLE CLAW

Militants seized the U.S. Embassy in Tehran, Iran, in November 1979. The militants took the Americans hostage. They held the hostages captive inside the U.S. Embassy. The Air Commandos were assigned to help rescue the Americans. The Air Commandos would support other special forces, who would fight their way into the embassy. The mission was called Operation Eagle Claw. It was a night operation. The Air Commandos wore night-vision goggles. On the flight to Tehran, to keep from being seen, they covered the landing lights on their aircraft. They used only a few infrared lights at the desert refueling site. They had practiced landing in the desert at night. But it was so dark that a helicopter crashed into an airplane. The helicopter and the plane were destroyed. Eight Americans were killed. The mission failed, even before the rescue force got to Tehran.

The United States strengthened the Air Commandos and other special forces in the 1980s.

in Kuwait in 1991. They saw action in Afghanistan starting in 2001 and in Iraq beginning in 2003. They work wherever they are needed. That is why their motto is Any Time, Any Place.

CHAPTER THREE: ANY TIME, ANY PLACE

The Air Commandos have very special roles to play. And many of those roles go beyond the U.S. Air Force. Air Commandos support every branch of the U.S. military. This is what makes them valuable. Many of the Air Commandos' actions are done secretly. Air Commandos want as little publicity as possible. They engage in many types of warfare quickly and efficiently. They must know about not only aircraft but also weapons, medicine, and ground combat.

Air Commandos in Special Tactics units differ from regular infantry soldiers. PJs perform reconnaissance and identify enemy targets. They can help rescue troops trapped in enemy territory. All PJs are trained medics. CCTs usually arrive by air, then work on the ground. They coordinate attacks against enemy targets. They direct aircraft during combat, like air traffic controllers at airports. They prepare safe landing areas. They might work with other military forces, like the U.S. Army or Marines, during these attacks.

CCTs survey a field during the 2010 mission in Haiti to set up a site for future air drops.

MISSION IN FOCUS

RESCUE IN HAITI

Not all Air Commandos' missions are military. The country of Haiti was nearly destroyed by an earthquake on January 12, 2010. Air Commandos went to Haiti immediately. They coordinated all the aircraft bringing rescue supplies and volunteers. They had to communicate with people who spoke many different languages, such as French and Creole. They had to get thousands of pounds of food, medical supplies, and volunteers to different parts of Haiti. By February 24, 2012, the Air Commandos had helped deliver 8,500 pounds (3,860 kilograms) of medical supplies, 9,500 pounds (4,310 kg) of food and water, and seventy-three thousand hand-cranked radios to people all over Haiti. Other Air Commandos moved debris and rescued trapped earthquake victims.

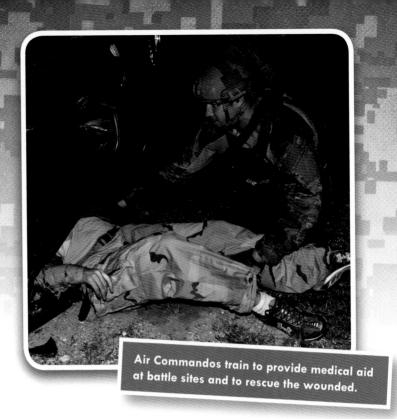

Air Commandos train to provide medical aid at battle sites and to rescue the wounded.

Sometimes Special Tactics units are on the ground fighting. Helicopter and airlift crews secretly drop Air Commandos and supplies into areas guarded by hostile troops. Then they come back and pick them up again when the work is done. Air Commandos also find individual people and help rescue them—or capture them. And they help track down terrorists quickly and quietly.

Air Commandos jump out of aircraft into enemy territory without being seen. They can create a landing field in almost any terrain. They guide aircraft to land safely in any weather. They also direct planes with laser-guided bombs and missiles to enemy targets. They use laser beams to mark locations where enemies are hiding. This helps laser-guided bombs hit the right target.

Air Commandos are experts at search and rescue techniques. Pararescue jumpers come in on helicopters. They can climb down ropes or be lowered by steel cables to reach a wounded soldier.

Air Commandos practice fast-roping from a helicopter.

PJs practice using a hoist to rescue the wounded.

Meteorology is a vital Air Commando role as well. Special Operations Weather Team members must pass all the usual Air Commando training and learn specialized meteorology skills too. Weather information is critical for planning missions and keeping aircraft safe in the sky.

The Air Commandos' techniques and tactics are partly based on their modern equipment. They use the world's best aircraft. Air Commandos in Special Operations Wings man gunship airplanes to fire on enemy ground forces. They can fly so close to the ground that they have to dodge trees and buildings.

The Air Commandos are in greater demand than ever before. Their ability to help find terrorists and other hostile groups makes them very important in places such as Afghanistan.

NIGHT STALKERS

A new group of army pilots and aircrew, the U.S. Army 160th Special Operations Aviation Regiment (SOAR), was created in 1981. These pilots became experts at flying helicopters anywhere in any weather but especially at night. They have advanced equipment for radar, navigation, evasion, and communication. This group is known as the Night Stalkers because they can fly at night as easily as other aircraft can during the day.

CHAPTER FOUR: GETTING THE JOB DONE

The Air Commandos are successful because of their skills and training. They know how to do their jobs very well. But another part of their success is the equipment they helped develop.

Air Commandos have very specialized equipment. Some of their most important tools are high-tech aircraft. The CV-22 Osprey aircraft combines the best parts of an airplane and a helicopter. Its propellers allow it to take off vertically like a helicopter. But in the air, its wings rotate so it flies like an airplane. This gives it greater speed and range than a helicopter. Helicopters such as the MH-60 Black Hawk drop troops and supplies. Other helicopters broadcast messages from loudspeakers during emergencies or send radio and television signals.

The AC-130J Ghostrider gunship is used for precision attacks. Sensors allow the aircraft to identify whether forces on the ground are friends or foes. The sensors use visual and electronic information and work in all types of weather.

Refueling planes can pump gas through long hoses to other planes while in the air. This keeps pilots from having to land in order to refuel.

The CV-22's propellers can rotate forward during flight, allowing the aircraft to fly faster.

UNIFORMS

Air Commandos usually wear the U.S. Air Force uniform. Called the Airman Battle Uniform, this clothing has a tiger-stripe camouflage pattern. Air Commandos also wear a special patch on the pocket of their combat uniform. In addition, some Air Commandos wear a distinctive beret. PJs wear a maroon beret. CCTs wear a scarlet beret. Special Operations Weather Team members wear a gray beret.

Combat controllers provide support as an MC-130 Combat Talon airplane takes off.

The MC-130, or Combat Talon, airplane delivers Air Commandos and other troops into combat areas, picks them up, and also drops supplies. The MC-130J Commando II is a state-of-the-art plane designed for AFSOC. It refuels helicopters and the CV-22 Osprey in midair. Airborne Warning and Control System (AWAC) planes are like mobile command centers high in the air. AWACs can monitor ground activity as well as coordinate communications.

Aircraft are, of course, among the most vital kinds of equipment for Air Commandos. Many Air Commandos pilots are trained to fly foreign-built aircraft. They can also fly older U.S. aircraft that are still used in other countries. But pararescue jumpers have other special tools as well. Every PJ carries a medical kit. Each kit is packed identically. One PJ can use another's kit easily if he has to. A PJ can even use his kit in the dark.

A PJ inspects equipment used for mountain climbing and survival.

Air Commandos on the ground have to carry survival equipment, communications equipment, and weapons. The weapons they use include M9 9-millimeter pistols with silencers, shotguns, M203 grenade launchers, M4 carbines, and M249 machine guns. They also carry laptop computers with radios for receiving intelligence and coordinating attacks. Commandos sometimes carry loads of more than 160 pounds (73 kg). Among the heaviest things they carry are batteries for their radios and electronic devices.

Special Tactics members must be able to use any piece of technology from any branch of the military. They use weapons guidance systems to mark locations for attack. They use small, unmanned aerial vehicles (UAVs), sometimes called drones. UAVs are flown by remote control over enemy territory. They have cameras to gather information.

Air Commandos use small inflatable rubber boats with outboard motors, such as the Zodiac, to travel on water. The Rescue All Terrain Transport (RATT) is a modified dune buggy. The RATT is used on the battlefield to move people, equipment, and wounded troops. But an Air Commando's greatest asset is not a gadget or an aircraft. It is the training and knowledge every Air Commando must have.

"Often our [Air Commando] folks are working . . . and no one even knows we're in the country."

—Lieutenant General Michael W. Wooley, former commander, U.S. Air Force Special Operations Command

PJs practice using a Zodiac boat for water rescues.

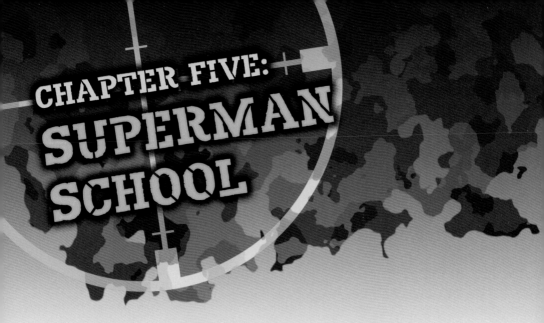

CHAPTER FIVE: SUPERMAN SCHOOL

Only airmen with talent and dedication become Air Commandos. They need many different skills. They must learn to use the equipment and weapons of modern warfare. They need survival skills if they are alone in unfamiliar territory. They must be in excellent physical shape. They need to have courage. They form close bonds with other Air Commandos. But even the bravest, most physically fit, smartest airmen do not always make it into the Air Commandos.

Recruits for the Air Commandos Special Tactics units are members of the regular air force. At this time, only men can join the Air Commandos. They have to pass several tests to be accepted for training. These tests

"The [Air Commandos] take higher risks to accomplish higher gain."
—Captain Paul Pendleton, MC-130 Combat Talon navigator

Recruits must pass difficult training to become Air Commandos.

are called the Physical Abilities and Stamina Test (PAST). Recruits must swim underwater for 82 feet (25 m) without taking a breath. Then they swim above water for 1,640 feet (500 m). If they stop at all, they fail. Then they must run a mile and a half (2.4 kilometers). This is followed by push-ups, sit-ups, and pull-ups. Recruits must meet high standards for running speed and strength.

Airmen practice jumping into the ocean from a C-130 Hercules aircraft.

Few airmen make it all the way through the PAST. Those who do also need official letters from three superior officers. These letters must recommend them for the Air Commandos. Then the airmen must write essays about why they want to be Air Commandos.

CCTs and PJs go through similar training. CCTs call their two years of training the Pipeline. PJs start with an indoctrination course commonly called Superman School. During this nine weeks, recruits are tested to their physical limits. They also begin weapons and medical training. Technical training continues at PJ University, or PJU. Throughout training, PJs and CCTs are deprived of sleep, food, and rest, and are put under more stress. This teaches them to endure difficult situations.

Recruits learn about navigation, shooting, and scuba diving. This training is followed by parachute lessons. Finally, they have survival training in the wilderness. They learn to make fires, find food and water, build shelters, climb mountains, and go down steep cliffs.

HELICOPTER ESCAPE

One part of Air Commandos' training is learning how to escape aircraft that have crashed into the water. Recruits are strapped into seats in a model helicopter. The helicopter is dropped into a swimming pool and turned upside down. Recruits have to escape and swim to the surface.

Air Commandos practice combat scuba diving at Hurlburt Field in Florida.

Air Commandos are honored for their bravery in combat.

PJs learn to treat injuries and illnesses. They become experts in parachuting. CCTs learn all about aircraft and aircraft control. They practice organizing a mission command center for aircraft, like an air traffic control tower at an airport. They practice parachuting into dangerous areas. They learn to set up secret airstrips for airplanes to land. Then CCTs and PJs come together for the intense Advanced Skills Training course. This yearlong final training step prepares them for real-world action.

The men who make it through the Air Commandos training are ready to both fight and rescue. They can work with every other military group in any situation. They put themselves at risk and don't wait to see if things are perfectly safe. There are many men who want to become Air Commandos. Only a few will be accepted to start the training. Even fewer make it through. It is a difficult and stressful job. But in today's world, Air Commandos are needed more than ever. They are carrying out more missions in more places around the world than ever before.

They help evacuate Americans from embassies in dangerous places such as Liberia. They helped enforce a no-fly zone over Iraq. They helped rescue stranded U.S. Army Rangers in Somalia. They set up airfields to bring humanitarian aid to the people of Rwanda. They help track down terrorists and other criminals who might harm Americans. They are ready to protect American citizens and military men and women . . . Any Time, Any Place.

Air Commandos are always ready to come to the rescue.

ALLIED FORCES
friendly nations that often help one another in wars; in World War II, the twenty-six countries, including the United States, that fought against the Axis powers (Germany, Italy, Japan, and others)

CIVILIAN
a person not serving in the military

EVACUATE
to move someone from a dangerous place to a safe one

GUNSHIP
an airplane or helicopter heavily armed with machine guns, cannon, missiles, and rockets for attacking enemy targets on the ground

MEDIC
a soldier who is specially trained to give first aid in combat

RECONNAISSANCE
secret information gathering

ROTATING BEACONS
small, bright flashing lights that can be seen for 20 miles (32 km)

SMOKE GRENADE
a grenade the shape of a soup can that gives off thick smoke as it burns

TALIBAN
militant Islamic movement of Pashtun tribesmen from around Afghanistan

TERRAIN
the physical features of a piece of land

LEARN MORE

Further Reading

David, Jack. *Air Force Air Commandos.* Minneapolis: Bellwether Media, 2009.

Lusted, Marcia Amidon. *Army Rangers: Elite Operations.* Minneapolis: Lerner Publications Company, 2014.

Porterfield, Jason. *USAF Special Tactics Teams.* New York: Rosen Central, 2008.

Websites

Air Force Special Operations Command

http://www.afsoc.af.mil/aircommandos.asp

This is the official website of the Air Commandos. Find photos and recruiting information here.

National Museum of the Air Force

http://www.nationalmuseum.af.mil/education/kids/index.asp

Learn about aviation, the air force, and air force vocabulary through the museum's website, which includes interactive activities and puzzles.

Official Website of the U.S. Air Force

http://www.af.mil

The official U.S. Air Force website includes news and information. Learn all about this branch of the U.S. military here.

INDEX

About the Author

Marcia Amidon Lusted has written more than seventy-five books for young readers. She is also a magazine editor, a writing instructor, and a musician.

WITHDRAWAL